The Life of a Saint

John Mary Vianney
The Holy Curé of Ars

Text: Sophie de Mullenheim – Illustrations: Adeline Avril

Translated by Janet Chevrier

Ignatius

MAGNIFICAT

To Become a Priest!

A tree branch cracked. The little troop stopped and listened to the noises of the night. After a few moments, Mathieu and Marie Vianney set off again in silence, with their six children following behind.

"Shh!" whispered one of the boys, John Mary,* to his sister Marguerite.

"My feet hurt", whimpered the little girl.

"Here," suggested her brother, "take my hand. We're almost there."

In the distance, he could make out the shape of the farmhouse in the shadowy light.

---

* Jean-Marie, in French

$\mathcal{A}$nd a few minutes later the whole Vianney family was indeed gathered together in a back room of the building along with many other families. A priest stood in the middle of the room celebrating Mass. Everyone had come there in secret, having faced many dangers to keep this nighttime appointment with the Lord. For this was the time of the French Revolution, when many priests were hunted down and thrown into prison or killed. Mass was forbidden. Churches were closed. Crosses were destroyed. And yet, men and women went on praying and going to Mass.

In front of the makeshift altar, John Mary said the Our Father in Latin along with those around him. *"Pater noster, qui es in caelis, sanctificetur nomen tuum ... "* John Mary was seven years old. He had not made his First Communion yet, but his love for the Lord was already immense. For some time now, a deep desire had been growing in his heart—he wanted to become a priest!

$\mathcal{B}$ut until he could make his dream come true, John Mary had to help at home. Every day, he and his sister Marguerite would lead the flock of sheep into the valley. While watching over the sheep and knitting woolen socks, he would tell his sister stories from the Bible that his mother had taught him.

When he had finished, he would run to the stream to pray. Then he would take a little statue of the Virgin Mary out of his pocket, place it in the hollow of a tree, and begin his prayer.

This little statue of the Blessed Virgin never left his side. His mother had given it to him as a present because he had agreed to give his pretty rosary beads to Marguerite. John Mary loved his little statue so much, he even slept with it.

One day, his parents found him in the barn. Clasping the statue of the Virgin to his heart, the little boy was so deep in prayer that he had forgotten dinnertime!

To be a priest! That was John Mary's fondest dream when he grew up. But it was very hard to make this dream come true. To become a priest, it was not enough to love the Lord with all your heart. You also had to know Latin in order to read the Scriptures. And, unfortunately, John Mary was not very good at school.

"Conjugate the Latin verb 'to love' in the past subjunctive", Father Balley quizzed him.

"*Amavissem, amavisses …*

"Oh, John Mary!" exclaimed the priest, losing his patience. "Concentrate!"

"Yes, Reverend Father. I'm sorry. I got that wrong. *Amarem?*"

"No, no, no!" grumbled the priest. "*Amaverim, amaveris …* Come, come! We already went through this yesterday!"

"I'll never get it right", John Mary said in despair.

"Courage, my boy", said Father Balley in a kindlier tone. "Don't forget that I accepted you in my class because I know you'll make a good priest. For years now, you've made progress, step by step. Now is not the time to give up."

John Mary sighed. He had already failed the exam once. He got mixed up and gave the wrong answers to the questions. It was a good thing Father Balley was there; the priest begged that John Mary might be allowed to take the exam again. It was very unusual, but the priests on the examination board agreed to it.

John Mary bravely went back to his books and worked and worked until at last, on the day of the exam, he gave all the right answers. But the vicar general in charge of the examination board wanted to know a little more.

"This John Mary Vianney, does he pray often and well?" he asked Father Balley.

"To perfection!"

The vicar general scratched his chin, closed his eyes, and thought for a moment. At last, he looked up and smiled. "Well, then," he announced, "I accept him for the priesthood! The grace of God will do the rest."

John Mary Vianney's dream had come true! He was ordained a priest in 1815 at the age of twenty-nine and was sent to the parish of Écully, near the city of Lyon, France, alongside dear Father Balley!

The Village of Ars

There was lively talk in the village square.

"Have you seen the new curé?" asked one villager.*

"I hear he's called John Mary Vianney", answered another. "He looks pretty young to me."

"Little Antoine Givre met him first", one woman told them. "He showed the curé the road to the village, and the curé said to him, 'You've shown me the road to Ars; I'll show you the road to heaven.'"

A man standing in the doorway of the coffee shop sneered, "Ha! The road to heaven! The curé's going to have his work cut out for him!"

* A "curé" is the word for a parish priest in France.

It has to be said, the people of the village did not love the good Lord very much. Ever since the Revolution, people hardly ever heard him mentioned anymore. The inhabitants of Ars preferred going drinking, dancing, and having fun, rather than praying.

And yet, almost everyone went to the new priest's first Mass. Mostly out of curiosity.

"He's not very tall", whispered one man to an old lady. "And not very good looking, either. And his cassock is all frayed."

"I'm not surprised", said the woman. "It seems there's nothing left in the rectory—he's given everything away. Even his bed!"

"Shh!" complained the woman next to her. "Keep quiet and listen to him!"

And something incredible happened. The new Curé of Ars said the Mass so earnestly, he spoke so gently, and he prayed so beautifully that many of the parishioners were deeply moved. They left the church after that Mass completely transformed.

"Our church may be a poor one," one of them remarked, "but our priest is a saint."

In a few months, the village of Ars had changed completely. The good priest knew each one of the inhabitants; he took time to talk to everyone, to invite them to come to Mass or go to confession. No one was left out, not even the little orphan girls for whom he opened a school called "Providence".

In his sermons, he called on each and every one of them to stop their drinking and silly amusements and to respect the Lord.

One Sunday, he came across a strange wagon on the road: a horse cart filled with hay was moving along without a driver! Having spotted the priest in the distance, the driver had hidden. He knew that anyone working on a Sunday could expect a gentle scolding from the priest.

"Hold on," thought John Mary, "I recognize those horses. Stop hiding, my friend", he called. "I know who you are."

$\int$heepishly, the man came out of his hiding place.

"Good day, Reverend Father", he mumbled.

"I've really caught you this time, my friend! But remember that, even if I hadn't seen you, God sees you always!"

The man decided not to work on Sundays anymore. And he was not the only one. The parishioners listened to their priest more and more.

The Curé of Ars did not want anything for himself. He slept on the floor with a stone for his pillow. He would often skip meals. If someone gave him a present of a new pair of shoes, he would give them to a poor person and go on wearing his old worn-out boots.

On the other hand, he wanted all the most beautiful things for God. He would travel as far as Lyon in order to buy vestments to celebrate Mass.

"What do you think of this chasuble, Father?" asked the shopkeeper, showing him a vestment embroidered all in gold.

"No! It's not beautiful enough. Nothing is beautiful enough for God!"

One generous donor even sent him religious objects all the way from Paris!

"How beautiful!" exclaimed the parishioners, as they opened up the wooden crates.

"Beautiful", agreed the good priest. "But in heaven, everything will be even more beautiful!"

The church was transformed, too. Father Vianney decorated it and enlarged it, paying for all the work himself.

"This church won't be able to hold all the people who will come here one day", he thought.

And Father Vianney was right! Soon the little church was too little. But then, the people of the village were not the only ones who went to church in Ars. People came from all over to attend Mass. For no one celebrated Mass like this good priest. His love for Jesus was so strong, it showed in everything he did. He made the Lord present and alive for everyone.

People would line up all the way down the street until late at night
to make their confession to him. In the midst of the crowd, the Curé
of Ars could spot those who needed him most. One day, he went out
to find a woman who had not been able to get into the church.

"You, madam, you're in a hurry", he said. "Come quickly to make
your confession."

The woman was astonished. How could this priest whom she had
never seen before know that she had sixteen children waiting for
her at home? God had given Father Vianney the gift of seeing into
people's hearts. Miracles even happened in his presence.

There was in fact another woman in need of the Curé of Ars. It was Mrs. Dévoluet. She had left her son, who was unable to walk, with a family in the village while she went to confession. The priest noticed her in the crowd.

"Come", he said to her. "You have the least time to spare!"

Mrs. Dévoluet went with the priest, made her confession, and left, forgetting to talk to him about her son.

"Oh, how stupid of me!" she thought.

Quickly, she ran to get her child and brought him back for the priest's blessing.

"That child's too big for you to be carrying him like that", he said. "Put him down."

"But he can't walk!"

"He will. Go pray before Saint Philomena."

The priest kissed the little boy, who then with difficulty managed to walk as far as the chapel of Saint Philomena. An hour later, all at once he stood up, exclaiming, "I'm hungry!"

And with that he ran to the door, where he suddenly stopped. It was raining outside, and he did not have any shoes on. For what good would it have done him to wear shoes, since he could not walk?

A Life of Sacrifice

In his confessional, the good curé would shiver in the cold or suffocate in the heat. His wooden bench was hard, but he refused to use a cushion. He would have hunger pangs, since he rarely took time to eat. The Curé of Ars did not want to lose a minute. There was so much work to be done, so many people to bring to the love of God!

The curé's day began very early. Sometimes he would be in the confessional as early as one o'clock in the morning! For six or seven hours, he would sit and listen, advise, comfort, and offer God's forgiveness. Next, he would celebrate the Mass with all his heart; then he would return to the confessional or to catechism.

At lunchtime, there would be so many people in the church and in the village square that it took him a long time to get home. Sometimes they crowded around him so tightly that he almost suffocated. But Father Vianney had a clever idea— he threw a handful of medals up in the air. The people ran to pick them up, and the priest was at last able to slip back into the rectory. Phew!

Father Vianney had only an hour for lunch. He would quickly eat a few boiled potatoes, which served as his meal, and then use the little time left to get a bit of sleep, tidy his room, or visit the sick. And he would pray, too, in the silence of his room. By one o'clock, the Curé of Ars would be back at church … until nine o'clock in the evening. What a schedule!

On July 30, 1859, when he was seventy-three, the Curé of Ars was still in his confessional at one o'clock in the morning! But his voice was getting weak, his speech was impossible to understand. Completely exhausted, he went home to bed. During the night, he asked for a priest.

"I'm going to call the doctor", the woman looking after him said hurriedly.

"There's no point", responded the curé in a frail voice. "The doctor can't do anything."

The end was near, and he knew it.

Horrified at the idea of losing their priest, the parishioners rushed to the rectory. They jostled each other in the stairway and crowded onto the landing, trying to see him one last time.

On August 4, 1859, John Mary Vianney gave up his soul to God. Ars had lost its dear curé. The church bells tolled. Men and women came from all over to pay him their last respects. Six thousand people traveled to his burial! And the bishop and three hundred priests were there as well.

For all of them, the Curé of Ars was already a saint. The way he celebrated Mass, his great kindness to all who came to him for confession, the miracles he had caused, the beauty of his teachings—all these things had led to the fame of this modest little curé all around the Lyon region. His fame was so great that, in 1925, he was proclaimed a saint. Everyone was to learn of the wonders achieved by this man.

The boy who had had such trouble learning Latin became the patron saint of priests, first in France and then of "all parish priests throughout the world"!

What Saint John Mary Vianney once predicted has never ceased to be true—the little church of Ars is not big enough to hold all those who go there.

Pilgrims have continued flocking to the little village ever since the death of the good curé. Of course, they no longer go to see the curé the way they used to. But they go to Ars to ask Saint John Mary Vianney to pray for them from heaven.

Feast Day

Saint John Mary Vianney's feast day is August 4, the anniversary of the day of his death.

The Patron Saint of All Priests

More than anything else, Saint John Mary Vianney loved to say Mass. He would often say:
"There is nothing greater than the Eucharist."
He also wanted to help his parishioners progress and to become closer to Jesus through confession and prayer.
It was for this great faithfulness and his holiness of life that he was beatified in 1905 and declared the patron
of the priests of France. He was proclaimed a saint in 1925 by Pope Pius XI. In 1929, Saint John Mary Vianney became
the "patron saint of parish priests throughout the world."
Pope John Paul II visited Ars in 1986. The seminary of Ars was opened in 1988.
The seminary is a school for the formation of young men who wish to become priests.

The Sanctuary of Ars

In Ars, you can still see the rectory where Saint John Mary Vianney lived as well as the "monument of the encounter",
which commemorates the spot where the Curé of Ars met the little boy who showed him the road to Ars.
You can also see the church where Saint John Mary Vianney prayed, celebrated Mass, and heard confessions.
After his death, it was enlarged by the extension of a great basilica.
The 450,000 pilgrims who visit each year can gather there.
And finally, you can visit the wax museum, which displays different scenes from the life of the holy curé.

Saint Philomena

Philomena was a girl of twelve or fifteen who died as a martyr in the time of the first Christians.
In 1835, Pauline Jaricot, the founder of the Society for the Propagation of the Faith, went to Mugnano, Italy,
to venerate Saint Philomena's relics.
She returned home cured of the illness that had kept her confined to a chair. She brought some of Philomena's relics back
to Lyon with her and, a few years later, gave them as a gift to John Mary Vianney, who had become her friend.
Saint John Mary Vianney was often to invoke the aid of Saint Philomena.

The Universal Call to Sainthood

"I will show you the road to heaven!" These words,
spoken by the Curé of Ars to the little boy who showed him the road to Ars,
express his desire to help everyone follow the road of holiness toward God.
For him, to be a priest meant "to give God to men and men to God."